D1044849

Bette Bao Lord

Novelist and Chinese Voice for Change

Bette Bao Lord
Novelist and Chinese Voice for Change

By Mary Virginia Fox

Consultant: Parris H. Chang, Ph.D.
Professor of Political Science
Director, Center for East Asian Studies
The Pennsylvania State University
University Park, Pennsylvania

CHILDRENS PRESS®
CHICAGO

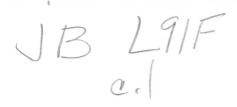

PICTURE ACKNOWLEDGMENTS
AP/Wide World Photos—pages 4, 88, 98
Permission Courtesy of Bette Bao Lord—pages 8, 18 (3 photos),
28, 54 (2 photos), 55, 56 (2 photos), 57 (2 photos), 58, 60 (3 photos),
61 (2 photos), 62 (2 photos)
People Weekly © 1981 Evelyn Floret—page 59
Cover illustration by Len W. Meents

Project Editor: Mary Reidy
Designer: Karen A. Yops

Library of Congress Cataloging-in-Publication Data
Fox, Mary Virginia.
   Bette Bao Lord: novelist and Chinese voice for change / by
Mary Virginia Fox.
   p. cm.—(People of distinction)
   Includes index.
   Summary: A biography of the Chinese American author whose
own background and marriage to the American ambassador to China
has enabled her to help bridge the gap between the two cultures.
   ISBN 0-516-03291-7
   1. Lord, Bette—Biography—Juvenile literature. 2. Novelists,
American—20th century—Biography—Juvenile literature. 3. Chinese
Americans—Biography—Juvenile literature. [1. Lord, Bette.
2. Authors, American. 3. Chinese Americans—Biography.] I. Title.
II. Series: People of distinction biographies.
PS3562.0678Z65 1993
813′.54—dc20
[B]
                                                         92-36805
                                                             CIP
                                                              AC

TABLE OF CONTENTS

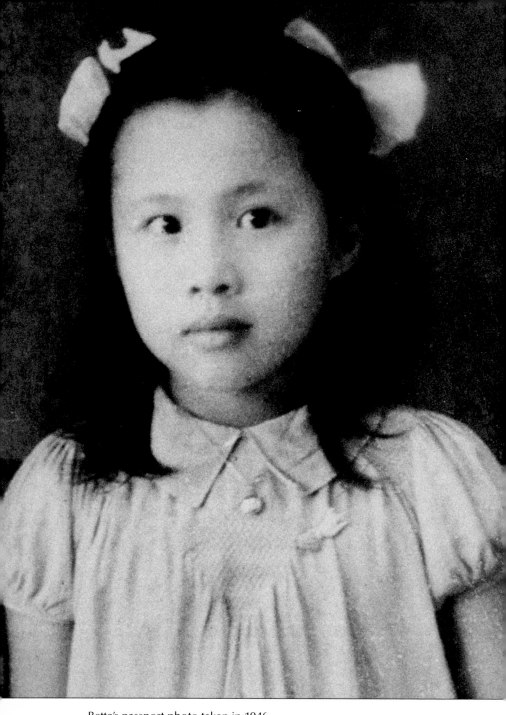

Bette's passport photo taken in 1946

Chapter 1

BORN UNDER THE SIGN OF THE TIGER

One of the very first things Dora Fang Bao did after giving birth to her daughter was to call in a fortune-teller. There was no better person than Whai Kung, the child's own grandfather. Whai Kung was well known as a brilliant poet and calligrapher and as a doctor who prescribed herbs for the ailing. He also was known for his uncanny accuracy in telling a person's future.

Whai Kung carefully studied the space between the baby's eyebrows, the length of her earlobes, and the shape of her head. He also consulted charts and maps of the stars at the exact time of the baby's birth.

The baby was born in 1938, the year of the tiger, at three in the morning. It was important to note the time to determine the strength of the rule of the tiger. In addition, the child's mother had been born under the same sign; and finally, the infant shared the same birthday as her father and his father, November 3. With so many favorable omens, it was said that the child would have a full life with nothing to fear.

Her spirits would be strong. These invisible spirits, like a fairy godmother, were believed to be the guiding forces that would direct her destiny, as a protection against adversity.

Dora Bao knew that it was important that she select a suitable name for this honored daughter. The child's father had not been present at the birth. He had been sent on an important mission by the Nationalist government of China to the province of Hunan. The name the grandfather chose had deep meaning, which translated to "Cyprus by the Babbling Brook." Cyprus was selected because it is a tree that is evergreen throughout all seasons. The child's grandfather made calculations of the birth date and discovered that of the five elements—water, metal, fire, wood, and earth—water was missing. Since water is necessary for all life, Babbling Brook was part of the baby's name. But there was to be another name, one that was chosen by the mother—probably before leaving China for America. Chinese often have many names, a formal name, a nickname, a school name, a pen name, but the first to be uttered in the child's presence would be the most important one.

Dora Bao was a woman influenced by two cultures. Chinese philosophy and Chinese life-style were hers because of the place of her birth and her upbringing, but Western ways were beginning to seep into the most traditional of Chinese culture. Even this far away from Hollywood, California, Dora was aware of a different pattern of life, a pattern that seemed quite glamorous at the time. She revered her family lineage, but the name she chose was Bette—after Bette Davis. Bette Davis had just won the Academy Award as best actress in 1938 for her performance in the movie *Jezebel*.

Whai Kung recorded the name and again assured his own daughter that his grandchild's spirits would prove exceptionally strong. Whai Kung could hardly have imagined how strong those spirits would be. He could not have imagined or predicted a day when Bette Bao Lord and her husband Winston Lord would occupy the imposing quarters of the United States Embassy in Beijing to serve as representatives of the most powerful country in the world to the most populous country in the world. Whai Kung could not have guessed that this child would grow up to be a talented and sensitive writer, able to bridge the differences between two cultures and to take the best of each. As a writer and a fine amateur photographer, Bette would be able to interpret these differences to her audience and point out the differences in national temperament that often shape the course of diplomacy. If anyone had known this much about the future, it might have seemed too heavy a burden to place on such tiny shoulders.

On the day of Bette's birth, it was hard to believe there would be nothing for her to fear in the future. The year was 1938. The world was on the brink of war, but China had already suffered death and destruction by enemy fire. The Japanese were sending bombers into China every day, demolishing centuries-old buildings as well as modern defenses.

Bette's father, Sandys Bao, was in the middle of much of the bombing by the Japanese. He had been educated as an electrical engineer both in China and in England. Now during the war he was temporarily commissioned a colonel in the Nationalist army and sent to the mountainous province of Hunan to construct a power plant. Instead of being safe in the country, he found that the installation he was working on was a prime target for Japanese bombers. Bette's mother had begged to join him, but he felt she would be safer in the city close to her relatives. But the war was everywhere. Shanghai, where the Baos lived, was under siege as well.

One day when Dora Bao was out for a walk, carrying her baby in her arms, the air raid sirens sounded. People all around them scurried for the shelters, but Dora remained frozen on the spot with terror. Instead of running, she thrust her young child into the hands of a stranger who was heading for the safety of the shelter. Dora Bao stood alone in the street until the all clear sounded. Then she waited at the entrance of the shelter to retrieve Bette.

Such a story led Sandys Bao to agree that his family might be safer with him. He tried to prepare his wife Dora for the primitive conditions they would be forced to endure in the country. As a member of the scholarly house of Fang, Dora had been waited on by servants and privileged to share the life led by the scholars, doctors, artists, and philosophers of her family. Sandys Bao had an impressive background also, but he had become used to life in the hinterlands.

Dora asked for only one convenience. Could he please provide a portable potty they could take with them? It must have been a strange sight to see the beautifully dressed Dora carrying her baby, while her husband in Bermuda shorts led the way with a wooden potty-chair strapped to his shoulders.

The Baos were safe for a few weeks until the Japanese scored a direct hit on the power plant. For months they were forced to flee from place to place depending on the movements of the army. One of the stops was Guilin where Bette's sister, Cathy, was born.

The Baos lived above a hostel where American pilots who flew supplies to Chiang Kai-shek's army were quartered. Bette was now four years old, inquisitive and anxious to explore every inch of territory within her domain. She loved hearing the strange words the pilots spoke, but they made no sense to her. The men must have taken a liking to the precocious little girl, because never once did they scold her for ringing the borrowed school bell in their ears so they would wake up and give her another lesson.

Only once did her father spank her. That was for ignoring

the air raid siren on the first wail before following the others into the cold dark tunnel that she disliked.

When the end of the war came in 1945, the family headed home to be with aunts and uncles and grandparents. It was here that baby Sansan was born, and given the name meaning "third in the family." Now that the family had grown, it was more important than ever that Sandys find a suitable job to support them. In the days of their ancestors there would have been ample wealth for a comfortable life, but the war had changed many things, and it was up to Sandys to care for his own.

Sandys still worked for the Nationalist government, but now a fine opportunity was offered to him because of his education and his knowledge of languages; unfortunately, it paid a very low salary. He was to be sent by the Nationalist government of China to New York to buy heavy equipment to help rebuild the war-torn country of China.

There was just one problem. Sandys would have to go alone. In 1946 there were tight travel restrictions following World War II, and there was no way he could make the trip with a wife and three children. But the assignment carried prestige and he could not turn down such an opportunity. When he returned, he expected they would be able to settle in their own home compound.

There were tears when Sandys had to leave, but he promised he would be back within a year's time. Almost as soon as he arrived in the United States, he started making inquiries about sending for his wife and children. Travel permits were not easy to acquire. The government agency that employed him tried to discourage him, but already Sandys Bao had been away from his beloved wife while studying abroad, as well as during their wartime separations. He was determined to find some way that would let them be together.

He was told a government salary could not support a family in New York City. Sandys explained that they had lived on a stringent budget before. They could manage. Then the government pointed out what a difficult trip it would be for his wife, who knew some English but was not fluent in the language. Ships crossing the Pacific were often overcrowded, and with three small children to manage, the journey of more than a month would be too hard.

After many letters back and forth between mother and father and aunts, uncles, and grandparents, a compromise was reached. Travel arrangements would be made only for Bette and her mother. Cathy, who was four, and Sansan, who was not quite a year old, would be left with Dora's sister and her husband, who had no children of their own. They felt that eight-year-old Bette was old enough to benefit from such a trip. It would give her a chance to see a very different culture and a distant part of the world. And she was at the right age, they hoped, to learn English quickly.

Bette's mother would not listen to warnings that the move would be a disastrous one. Why would her husband, who had traveled in America, urge her to come? Dora was nervous, yes, but she was strong willed, and when she had set her mind to a course of action, there was no turning back. She would overcome all obstacles, or learn to put up with them. She was going.

Little Cathy was old enough to realize what was happening. She clung to her mother at every step. She started packing her own things to be sure she would be ready when the trip started. Dora tried to explain that Cathy would be staying with her aunt and uncle, and there would be grandparents and second and third cousins to play with, but Cathy's tears came in sobs while Dora's flowed silently.

Finally it was decided that Dora would take both Cathy and Bette with her. Her heart ached at the thought of leaving Sansan behind, but Sansan was too young to know what was happening. She cooed contentedly in the arms of whoever would pick her up.

Aunt Ah Yee held Sansan as the family gathered to say good-bye to Dora, Bette, and Cathy, who were about to board the *Marylinx*. The ship loomed huge at the dock. Dora waited to board until the last minute, and as the ship's whistle sounded an ominous warning, she gave Sansan one last hug and hurried her other two children up the gangplank. They stood at the railing as the ship inched away from its mooring. Cathy waved her doll. Bette tried to act with the dignity expected of a grown-up eight year old. Grandfather was standing very quietly on the dock in the midst of the noise and confusion of departure. He was dressed in a long gray silk gown topped by a fur-lined vest. On his head he wore a gentleman's fedora.

Bette knew she should feel sorry to be leaving home, but the excitement of seeing her father again and the strange world he described with such enthusiasm was enough to shut out sadness. She did not know this was the last time she would ever see her grandfather Whai Kung.

Dora and Sandys Bao with their oldest daughter in China

Above: Dora and Sandys Bao in Brooklyn
Left: A 1947 photograph of Bette Bao
outside her home in Brooklyn

Chapter 2

AN OCEAN CROSSED

At last the ocean ended at San Francisco. It seemed strange to have steady ground underfoot instead of the motion from the waves. There was no time for sightseeing in San Francisco. Dora was too anxious to get to New York to see Sandys and shed some of the frightening responsibilities of caring for her family in this strange country. They took a taxi to the train station, and three days later the children were being hugged by their father.

Dora stood behind smiling, but, showing the propriety of her upbringing, her greeting was formal. Again they squeezed into a taxi with all their belongings and headed for Brooklyn, which was to be their home.

Before their first night together was over, Sandys was coaching them in English. Dora had been practicing very hard ever since her husband had suggested that she would be coming to America.

Bette tried some of her father's words, but there were many she couldn't begin to pronounce no matter how hard she twisted her tongue. Her father explained they would have one day together to get used to their new neighborhood so their mother would know where to shop. But the very next day he would have to go to work and Bette would be going to school.

Would anybody be able to understand her, Bette wondered? Her father admitted she would be the only Chinese student in the school. That made her mother worry so she made special rules. Because Bette might be the only Chinese girl these children would ever meet, Bette would have to be exceptionally good, a fine scholar, and always on her best behavior. She would have to be the ambassador for all of China, at least in Public School Number 8 on Poplar Street in Brooklyn, New York, USA. That seemed like a tremendous responsibility for an eight year old, but Bette was determined she would manage. Hadn't her grandfather said that strong spirits were protecting her?

The next day Dora and Bette set out for school. Bette wished her father, who spoke so well, was with them, but he had appointments he couldn't break. The teacher first asked Bette how old she was, which her mother thankfully was able to understand and interpret. Bette raised ten fingers. If she had been in China that would have been correct. On the day Bette was born she was considered one year old, and another year was added to her age on every New Year's Day after that. Bette had been born in November, and two months later the new year of 1939 was celebrated, so Bette would have been considered two years old that year in China.

The teacher seemed surprised, but Bette checked carefully. That would have been the year of the Rabbit. Then came the Dragon, Snake, Horse, Sheep, Monkey, Rooster, Dog, and now it was the year of the Boar, making it ten.

The teacher, Mrs. Rappaport, explained that Bette would be entering fifth grade. When those words were translated Bette was sure a mistake had been made. She had had only three years of schooling in China. How could she ever make up two whole years when she couldn't even understand what anyone was saying? Neither Bette nor her mother wanted to argue with the teacher, who, after all, must know the American rules they were to follow.

Bette was by far the smallest student in the class. Everyone was friendly—a better word might have been curious. They asked her all kinds of questions, but as soon as it became evident that she could do little more than smile at their words, they left her to her own devices. The device she used most of the time was to hurry home as if she had something very important to do.

Later when Bette was asked what her life was like as a young immigrant, she answered, "[You had] to develop a thick skin, even to enjoy people laughing at you. You make mistakes in the new language and culture, but you learn from them."[1]

However, the public school system did have some help for Bette. She attended REI—or Rapid English Improvement—classes twice a day. Here there was just the teacher to please, and instead of making fun of the strange way words seemed to get twisted, the teacher was usually smiling and encouraging.

Within four months Bette was babbling the words that had seemed so strange to her on her first day of school. She still didn't understand most of the jokes the kids told. Often she was the last to laugh, or sometimes she laughed when she wasn't supposed to.

Both Bette's mother and father tried to keep their spirits up, but it was hard, especially for Dora Bao. She was wise, yet innocent, unable to cope with the modern conveniences her husband had provided for housekeeping. A washing machine was a monster that devoured clothes, she thought. But she was the guiding force in requiring the highest standards of deportment. That meant that once Mother had given an order, there was no question of disobeying. Today Bette remembers that she would never dream of defying her mother.

Every morning before Bette left for school, her mother gave her a most critical inspection. Hair must be brushed to a sheen, braids neatly fastened with clips, blouse stiff with starch, and shoes polished until Bette could see her face when she bowed to say good-bye before racing out the door.

The minute she was out of the door she stepped into a completely different world, but her mother's rules were to be kept at all costs. Bette loved to run and jump and skip along the sidewalk, but that would spoil Mother's sense of dignity, so only on special occasions did Bette allow herself the joy of dancing and pirouetting to school, and certainly not within sight of her mother.

Her father bent rules more easily, except when it came to schoolwork. He had lived under a very domineering father himself and he knew the sense of frustration when his wishes and feelings had been crushed. Sandys Bao had confided some of these moments to Bette, which made her love and respect her father even more, knowing that he hadn't always been so perfect.

Grandfather must have been a terror to live with, but Bette's father always spoke with respect about his parents. There had been moments of disobedience, Sandys admitted, but his only regret was the lack of understanding between two generations whose experiences had been so different. Sandys was a spirited man who realized that part of growing up is asserting oneself, and that is why he allowed Bette so much freedom when she was growing up.

Sandys had attended a primary school quite a distance

from his home. In the winter, it was an added chore to carry all of his books home every day. Most of the students locked their books in their desks at school, but when Sandys had asked his father for money to buy a lock, the request was denied. His father admonished him that he should be thrifty and not waste money for unnecessary expenditures.

One day when Sandys left his books at the school, they were stolen. Not daring to tell his father, he had to do without them, and his grades suffered. His father gave him a sound thrashing. To get even, Sandys decided to take the words of his father quite literally. If locks were such an unnecessary extravagance, the family could do without them too. He broke every lock in their house.

This was such a horrendous breach of discipline that twelve-year-old Sandys was banished from his home. However, Sandys was not turned out into the cold, harsh world without some protection. He was sent to a religious school run by Chinese Baptists in the southern city of Ningbo, the ancestral home of the Baos, a thousand lis away from Tianjin. (A *li* is approximately a third of a mile.)

Instead of it being a punishment, the move turned out to be a blessing. Sandys felt free. He was baptized a Christian and with encouragement from a caring group of people, he turned his energy toward studying, what his own father had always wanted from him.

After five years at Ningbo, Sandys entered Jiaotung College in Shanghai, one of the finest universities in the country. Here Bette's father received his degree in electrical engineering. He showed his superiority in other fields as well. He was captain of the championship basketball and diving teams. His most important title was Number One Debater of China. This he won by being able to debate in English as well as Chinese. In doing so, he was noticed by General Chiang Kai-shek, who was head of the Nationalist government. After placing high in competitive examinations, Sandys was selected to continue his studies abroad at London University.

Before leaving for his studies, Sandys had met Dora, the woman he wanted to marry. She was from the prestigious house of Fang, a beautiful young woman much sought after. Dora consented to wait for Sandys' return, and in 1938 they were married in the ballroom of Shanghai's tallest building. In spite of the fact that Japanese bombs were falling all around, it was a very elaborate affair, with both sides of the family gathering to give best wishes to the union.

Bette loved to hear the story and asked that it and other stories be repeated again and again. Family was extremely important, and one way to strengthen those ties was to tell stories of the past. Now that her mother and father had literally abandoned their lifeline to their Chinese roots, they both felt it was important to continue their Chinese way of life, so that their children would know the richness of their heritage. The Baos may have lived in a typically suburban and upwardly mobile neighborhood when they moved to New Jersey, but, "I had a very Chinese family life," Bette says. "It was not American in philosophy."[2]

One of the greatest gifts Bette and her family had was the great amount of time the family spent together. Some families foster closeness by vacationing together. Bette fondly remembers sitting at the kitchen table talking endlessly with her parents. It is something they still do when they are together. Conversation is an art, and Bette learned it at an early age, not just talking about everyday activities, but philosophizing about politics, foreign affairs, the differences between their native country and their adopted land, or whatever came to mind. It was never boring.

After about four months in America, Bette had learned enough English to be fluent, mainly because of her age. Children learn very quickly, especially if they are thrown into a situation where they *have* to speak the new language.

Her teachers were kind, but in such a strange way. Even before Bette could string words together to make proper sentences, Mrs. Rappaport was asking Bette's opinion on all kinds of subjects. It didn't seem to matter whether her opinions made much sense. It was just a way the teacher had of making everyone come up with ideas of their own.

When it became evident that everyone's thoughts were accepted even when really "far out"—a new expression Bette had just learned—it began to be fun to puzzle out solutions to old problems. In China, opinions were only welcomed when they coincided with the teachers', and the teachers remained teachers only as long as their opinions matched those of the government party leaders. It might be hard to get back to the old system once they returned.

Bette in Vermont in 1948

Chapter 3

BECOMING AN AMERICAN

No one spoke of returning to China. One month followed another. Sandys had heard reports, both in the American newspapers and from the Chinese officials where he worked, that a violent civil war was going on between the Communist forces of Mao Zedong and the Nationalist party.

Dora wrote her sister and begged her to leave the mainland and settle in Taiwan where there would be a chance of a reunion. But Ah Yee was sure that life would soon return to normal now that the civil war was over. Like many others, she had great hopes for the new government now that China at last was at peace with itself.

Chiang Kai-shek and his forces eventually fled to the island of Taiwan to set up an exile Nationalist government. The Communists established the People's Republic of China on the mainland. With Mao's victory in 1949, returning home became unthinkable for the Baos. Landowners, even the powerful house of Fang, were stripped of their property. Anyone having had connections with the Nationalist government was considered an enemy. Sandys Bao had been an important person in the Nationalist government. It was feared that he would be tried and sent to prison if he returned to mainland China.

They hoped a time would come in the not-too-distant future when Chinese politics would reverse itself and permit those with different views and backgrounds to live in peace together. In the meantime, it seemed better not to endanger their relatives back in Shanghai and Tianjin. If they received word from America they might be branded enemies of the state, but it meant abandoning little Sansan, never knowing what she was doing or how she looked as she was growing up. There was never a day when Dora Bao didn't long to hold her young daughter in her arms, to show her the bright new world they had discovered so far away from their own true home.

Sandys Bao also grieved, but he tried to hide his deepest feelings from his wife to bolster her own morale. He begged Dora to think only of the bright side of their exile. Life in the United States was good. Perhaps they did not have as many luxuries as they had enjoyed before the war, but he had been able to find at least part-time employment because of his knowledge of both languages, Chinese and English. Besides, there were fine schools for their children. That was more important than wealth. Dora quietly agreed. But never once did she give up hope that one day she would return for Sansan.

It was an obsession. At night when she tried to sleep she would lay out some wonderful plan to whisk her daughter away without the police even knowing she was gone, but in the morning she realized the scheme would never work and might even put her youngest daughter behind bars for life. It was a dread she could never put out of her mind.

In the meantime Bette took the job of becoming an American very seriously. She learned how to play stickball, with book bags for bases, a borrowed bat and ball, and a rooting section that included the entire neighborhood. She had friends now, but soon the family moved to better quarters in East Patterson, New Jersey, and a year after that, when Bette was ready to enter high school, they moved to a red brick house in Teaneck, New Jersey.

Each move always meant making new friends, sometimes a frightening necessity. If you looked different from everybody else, it seemed more important to be the same in every other way. What made some people more popular than others?

Today Bette explains, "As a child, you want to fit in, to play ball and go to dances, to conform. As you get older, you become more interested in your roots, in the mysteries of you. That leads you back to tradition—things that you were never taught but somehow know."[1]

The choice of homes was always guided by which school

district was best. Education was the key to success and happiness, Mr. and Mrs. Bao emphasized. Bette and her sister did not have to be forced to take advantage of what their new country had to offer. Bette was very active both in the classroom and in other activities. She planned to attend college and was already saving money for the years ahead.

At the age of twelve Bette had her first job as a cashier in a Chinese restaurant. She worked from 5:30 to 9:00 P.M. during the week, with longer hours on weekends. She looked older than her years. She was quite tall now and serious and dependable. She was proud of her job. It gave her her first feeling of independence. Although she was not exactly wealthy by teen standards, she had the luxury of spending a bit more on clothes and movies.

It was about this time that the Bao family embarked on their own rather disastrous experiment as restaurateurs. Neither Dora nor Sandys had had any experience in such matters. It meant both parents were away from their family more hours than they cared to be. Bette became housekeeper and cook for her younger sister Cathy.

There were times when Cathy called her bossy, but being a second mother to someone four years younger meant there had to be some bossing to keep the family schedule going smoothly. Bette admits that she and Cathy are closer now than they were as children.

Bette admits that she is neither neat, precise, nor well organized, as some have described her. But in her choice of written words, she is very creative. She likes to get things done. She sets goals for herself, and with her parents' encouragement in her early years she met those goals.

To earn more income, Bette was employed to address envelopes for an insurance company. She was an expert typist. She had won honors for her speed and accuracy—a skill she was to use later as a writer.

The first close friend Bette made in high school was named Dolores. In contrast to Bette's shiny black hair and black sparkling eyes, Dolores was blond and blue eyed. There were others who were smarter and prettier and had more cashmere sweater sets, Bette remembers, but no one was more popular than Dolores. She planned to become a nurse, and she was very active in her church youth group.

Suddenly, joining this church group seemed very important to Bette. Her father patiently agreed to drive his daughter twice a week to the Lutheran church where regular members of the confirmation class were being taught. Bette didn't quite understand the meaning of all that Martin Luther had written and hammered on the door of a church a long time ago, but she was aware that it was Dolores's faith in this message that set her apart and bound this group together.

Somehow Bette did not feel the pull that brought her a

sense of belonging. Soon her father was released from the burden of driving Bette to and from her catechism lessons. Dolores's friendship was still cherished, but Bette admits they haven't seen each other since graduation.

Actually Bette had become a leader in the school herself, and other students were seeking her out. She was elected secretary of the student council, and she was a member of the winning debating team, something that made her father very proud. She liked to stand before an audience and speak. She showed an unusual amount of confidence and maturity that even with her father's coaching was Bette's talent alone.

She was also active in school plays. Bette has always managed to slip a bit of drama into her life. Imagination, being another person, acting—all seemed to come naturally to her.

Bette's mother dreamed "the typical Chinese version of the American dream: my child the -ist: chemist, internist, physicist, biologist—in short, scientist."[2]

Bette admits she was influenced by a sense of the dramatic. She saw herself as a second Marie Curie, creating magic in the laboratory and winning a Nobel prize.

The big decision that was discussed at family gatherings was what college Bette would attend when high school was behind her. She had excellent grades. She had decided that she'd win that Nobel prize in chemistry. It seemed sensible to choose a school not too far away from home and one with a student enrollment that would not engulf a newcomer with a boisterous social calendar or with a cold academic atmosphere.

Tufts University seemed to fill the bill. It was located in Medford, Massachusetts, a suburb of Boston. It was a co-educational university with an undergraduate enrollment of just over five thousand. Bette applied to only one college and she was accepted. It was time to pack up for another chapter in her life.

Bette felt at home at Tufts and she took pride in being both American and Chinese. Sometimes she would wear Chinese tunics and trousers. Other times jeans matched her mood. Friends were anxious to know about her background, her upbringing, and what was happening in the mysterious East. Bette had no personal news to tell of the East. What was China like? What she remembered came more from the stories her mother and father told of the past.

Several important things happened in her freshman year. First, one of her professors steered her away from her chosen field of chemistry. Bette admits to having been a bull in a china shop in the class lab. Instead of failing the course she turned her major to history and political science. Dealing with people and ideas seemed to hold more interest than the rather dehumanized rules of the chemistry lab. The world would have to wait for a future Marie Curie from another source.

The second discovery was modern dance, particularly the dramatic interpretation with body movement displayed by Martha Graham. A friend gave Bette a ticket to a Graham concert in Boston. Bette had never seen anything like this before. She was fascinated. Even as she sat in the audience her own body wanted to stretch and turn to the music. Drama had always been a powerful part of Bette's life; now here was a very personal way to express emotion through the use of arms, legs, head, and torso—in short, her whole being.

The very next day Bette made inquiries about taking lessons. She was seventeen, old to take on the harsh training of a dancer, but Bette had always displayed determination and self-discipline. The hours she spent in practice were a joy, even though her body often reacted with aches and pains.

Bette became a star pupil. It is one of the creative outlets Bette pursued for the next twenty years. When she stopped, it was an abrupt decision. But many of Bette's interests have come about by accident and when put aside have been replaced by others of equal interest.

College was a period of enthusiasm and growth for Bette. Again she enjoyed debating, whether in a private discussion group or at a podium. She decided to continue her education in graduate school at the Fletcher School of Law and Diplomacy, a division of Tufts. Another important event, whether she knew it or not, was to happen. She met a handsome, boyish-looking young man in her world economics class. It was just an introduction, but later when they met again at a social mixer he invited her to dance.

Bette remembers, "Then [he] proceeded to ask, 'Have you encountered much racial discrimination in this country?' I was dumbfounded. I thought he was taking a...survey."[3]

Winston Lord, who was the young man, admits it wasn't exactly an impressive beginning.

At first glance they seemed like an unmatched pair. Winston's background had been so very different from Bette's. The dissimilarities of culture always are hard to meld. Then, too, Winston had been brought up surrounded by family. The Baos had been cut off from family ties. But here were two people attracted to each other by a mutual interest in foreign affairs. Winston had had a close encounter with such dealings through his mother, Mary Lord, who had served as the United States Ambassador to the United Nations.

Winston was born August 14, 1937 in New York City. No fortune-teller predicted his brilliant career, but as the son of Oswald Bates Lord, whose family inherited money from textile enterprises, and Mary Pillsbury Lord, whose grandfather, Charles Alfred Pillsbury, started the well-known flour mills in Minneapolis, he started with advantages. Winston attended an Ivy League prep school, but the zeal with which he applied himself had nothing to do with family fortunes. He graduated from Yale University *magna cum laude* and was first in his class at the Fletcher School of Law and Diplomacy at Tufts University.

Bette calls him a WASP, but with more than a hint of humor. He in no way symbolizes the haughty person of prejudice most often designated with that term.

Both young people were attracted to each other from the very beginning, but Bette wanted to test a bit of independence, to strike out on her own before she thought of marriage. She had worked hard for her college degree and had been urged by her teachers to continue her studies at the Fletcher School of Law and Diplomacy. She didn't want to throw away the honors she had received before putting her abilities to use in a paying job.

After she finished her graduate study, she looked around for a job as far away from home as possible. She wasn't running away from an unhappy home life or from Winston. Nothing could have been further from the truth. But Bette wanted to prove she could accomplish something on her own. "I was proud and did not want to marry him [Winston] without having made my mark."[4]

She would have liked to have applied for work in the foreign service of the U.S. state department, but as yet she was not an American citizen. Without an American passport it was impossible for her to travel abroad. About as far as she could go was either Alaska or Hawaii. Hawaii was her choice.

Bette bought a one-way ticket and arrived with fifty dollars in her pocket. She had no job. But Bette's impeccable credentials saved the day. She was hired almost immediately as an assistant to the director of the University of Hawaii's East-West Cultural Center. When she started the job she and the director were the entire office force. Soon Congress appropriated ten million dollars for the center and responsibilities mounted as they planned exchange programs for students and professionals. Bette's ability to speak to a large audience was also a plus for her career. Not only did she accomplish important office work, but she spent a great deal of her time talking before groups explaining the various projects the council was sponsoring. By the time Bette left her job two years later she was in charge of a department that included thirty-five people.

When she returned to the West, Bette was hired as an advisor to the program director of the Fulbright Exchange program, helping select professors to teach abroad. In the meantime Winston had served a brief army hitch and had joined the United States foreign service. This meant Winston would be traveling. Their separation had already been long enough. Bette had tasted independence. She knew she was capable of handling a career. She intended to pursue one, but there seemed to be no rush in making a job commitment.

Love came first. Winston proposed in 1962 and Bette immediately accepted.

Both families were delighted with the match. The Baos had never had a son, nor the Lords a daughter. The families have remained close to this day. It was the U.S. state department that now had to give its blessing. Bette had to prove that she would be a suitable wife. At first she thought this was nothing more than proving that she spoke English, paid her taxes, had not committed any crime, and could name the president of the United States.

The examiner proved to be a stern questioner. He explained that if he disapproved of the marriage, Winston would no longer be considered eligible for the foreign service. Bette's immediate reply was, "Winston could find another job, but not another me."[5]

Bette's spotless credentials were eventually accepted. The state department notified them that Winston's career would be limited because of his father-in-law's affiliation with the Taiwan government. Sandys was employed by Taiwan as their sugar expert and sugar representative in the International Sugar Council. Because of this, Winston Lord would never have anything to do with China or Taiwan policy. But there were other parts of the world where his talents could be used, so the wedding date was set, but not before another very exciting event occurred.

Chapter 4

REUNITING A FAMILY

Bette's mother had never given up her fight to bring Sansan to America. If China wouldn't give Sansan a proper education, America would. Dora Bao planned a complicated scenario to whisk her daughter away from Communist-controlled China. It was solely of her own design. Her husband and concerned friends, in whom she had confided, tried to dissuade her because they did not want her to be heartbroken if Sansan wanted to stay in China. It was known that many young people had been indoctrinated in the ideology of the new regime. But Dora Bao felt the time was right to try bold action.

During the early part of 1962, travel restrictions had been partially relaxed and hundreds of refugees were pouring into Hong Kong. If Sansan could get that far across the border, the rest might be easy, Dora hoped. It had taken a certain amount of intrigue and a great deal of patience, but it seemed almost possible that now the dream would come true.

To give Sansan a legitimate reason for coming to Hong Kong, Dora Bao feigned a serious illness. She wrote three letters addressed to Sansan in care of her grandmother, which were mailed by friends in Tokyo. The first letter spoke of a serious operation she was having in a Tokyo hospital. The next letter forwarded an actual newspaper article that announced that the government of Hong Kong was granting permission to Chinese mainland students to visit their families in Hong Kong during the summer vacations. The Hong Kong border authorities would allow students into the city during the period from July 5 to August 31. The third letter was sent to make arrangements for someone to accompany Sansan across the border. Sansan would first have to take the train from Tianjin to Canton by herself. The last leg of the journey might be the most dangerous, and Dora Bao was sending payment for an escort. Never once was any suggestion made that the United States would be Sansan's final destination.

After doing all that was possible from her side of the Pacific Ocean, Dora Bao boarded a plane in late June and flew to Hong Kong for the long wait. Miraculously Dora's plans worked. Sansan was able to persuade authorities that her dying mother wanted to see her daughter for the last time. True, Sansan never made contact with the hired escort, but once the permit was granted Sansan managed very well on her own. Nothing was going to keep her from being reunited with her real mother. Sansan had not even known that her aunt and uncle weren't her real parents until her grandmother had revealed the information a few months before.

When she stepped from the train into the crowded station, there must have been a moment of panic. How would mother and daughter recognize each other after all these years? But when Dora called out her daughter's name, Sansan rushed into her arms. It was only then that Sansan knew that her mother was not on the brink of death and that the operation had been part of the ruse for the escape.

The reunion took place on August 18, 1962. Dora and Sansan stayed a week in Hong Kong to wait for the next refugee boat to Taiwan where Sandys Bao was to join them. They had to stay in Taiwan until October before Sansan's visa was cleared.

On October 18 Bette was waiting anxiously at the international airport in New York City to greet her sister whom she had not seen in sixteen years. Would Sansan be jealous of Bette and Cathy who had had a chance to go to good schools, to have all the food they wanted, to wear fine clothes? Would Sansan understand that her family had wanted to return, scoop her up in their arms, and give her all of these things? Would it be hard to break the barriers of being strangers to each other?

Bette saw her mother and father first as they came through the terminal gate at the airport. Then Bette caught a glimpse of Sansan. There was no mistaking her. Bette had a strange feeling that she was seeing herself as if in a mirror, although on closer inspection Bette was the taller of the two. Also Sansan had the pallor of someone who had not had a nourishing diet over the years. Her hair was thin, brushed neatly away from her face, but there was a broad smile, coupled with infectious laughter that sent the two girls into each other's arms. The reunion was complete. Sansan immediately took her place as one of the family.

They didn't stop talking that first night in 1962 until early the next morning. There were so many blank spaces in their lives to fill in, so much family history to record, and so many plans for a bright future in a new country, a bright future Bette hoped she could share with Sansan.

Bette and Sansan had had such different lives. It was hard to imagine the physical hardships Sansan had had to endure. Sansan was part of a labor detail that carried human excrement as fertilizer to rice paddies and smelted scrap metal in a school yard furnace. At home she had lived with an aunt and uncle who seemed more interested in their own welfare than Sansan's. Sansan had been forced to get up before dawn to wait in line for food in the market. She chopped the wood, cleaned the house, and washed the clothes. Sometimes dinner wasn't much more than bread cakes made of corn cobs.

Bette wondered if she would have had the strength to withstand these hardships herself. Her Chinese heritage might have given her the strength of *ren,* what the Chinese call the ability to endure, but her American background would have made her want to rebel. Yet there had been few rebellious survivors during the time of the Chinese Cultural Revolution. Both girls had much to learn from each other.

One of the first orders of business was for Sansan to learn English. Sandys Bao spent a minimum of two hours a day with his youngest daughter. In her eagerness to try new expressions, "Keep cool" turned out to be "Keep chilly," and "I am in a pickle" turned out to be "I am in a cucumber."[1] Dora helped tutor Sansan in getting along with others. Sansan had to learn to be less suspicious of people. Her own innate sense of humor helped smooth the transition. The warm love and support she felt from her family was returned in many ways.

Sansan had arrived just in time to be part of her sister's wedding. Bette was busily involved with plans for her marriage to Winston Lord. The Lord/Pillsbury clan is a large, close-knit family circle. When it came time to make out the invitation list, it included a thousand names. The service was to be held at a Presbyterian church in Washington, D.C. While neither Bette nor Winston are regular churchgoers, they wanted a religious ceremony.

But where was the bride's family going to hold the wedding reception? How was any home, club, or restaurant going to be able to accommodate the crowd? This was where influential friends of the Baos came to the rescue. Sandys Bao had many close contacts with the Chinese Nationalist government. Arrangements were made to hold the reception in the Chinese Nationalist Embassy in Washington. It was an event attended by many of the most important and influential figures in Washington.

The bride was beautiful, the groom handsome. But what was more important, they matched each other's intellectual curiosity. Winston tends to be restless, Bette frequently masks her boundless energy in a cloak of serenity. There would be differences, but it was the beginning of a life that was to hold many surprises. It was to be a happy life, and an unpredictable one.

Chapter 5

RAISING A FAMILY

Washington was to be their home for the next few months. Bette was still a director of programming for the Fulbright Foundation. Winston had been appointed a member of the staff of the office of congressional relations department, concerned with political, military, and economic affairs. He was not a specialist in any one field, but a "generalist" who had to keep abreast of many topics. He was soon made director of planning and coordination for the state department.

It meant hours of research analyzing documents and interviews and writing a condensed summary of opinions, often inserting his own.

Winston was a bright young man whose career was on the rise. As Henry Kissinger once explained, "The policy-planning staff has top priority on the ablest young people in the Foreign Service."[1]

There were long hours, but Winston always saved time for home. He and Bette often discussed the world's current problems at the dinner table. Bette was well informed and very often helpful in putting matters in perspective, but she needed a project of her own.

Bette admits that some of the most important events in her life have occurred as unplanned happy accidents. One day she happened to meet a publisher at a social reception. She spoke to him of Sansan's experiences as a young girl in Communist China. There were no books in the West that gave a look at China from an ordinary person's viewpoint. Here was a book just waiting to be written. The publisher encouraged Bette to find someone to write the story.

Bette didn't know any authors who spoke Chinese, so being very foolish, as she now recalls, she quit her job at the Fulbright office to write the story herself. She first started taping monologues by Sansan, then she added her own questions in interviews. As she translated the tapes from Chinese to English, she accumulated more than 250 pages of notes. These began to fall into an outline, and from then on the writing went more smoothly than she expected. Still there were many revisions before both she and Sansan were satisfied. Bette admits she had never intended to become a writer. Writing doesn't come easily for her, she says, perhaps because she is such a perfectionist.

Another special event was about to take place. Bette and Winston were expecting their first child. Bette wanted to finish the manuscript before the baby arrived. As she remembers, it was a race against time. The manuscript was delivered just a few days before Elizabeth Pillsbury Lord was born on March 24, 1964.

The book entitled *Eighth Moon* was published by Harper & Row. It was a great success. It has since been translated into fifteen languages and is frequently part of students' reading programs. The book is a shocking disclosure of the harsh life people had to endure during the Cultural Revolution. It is sensitively written and shows the courage and humor that enabled Sansan to endure such a seemingly hopeless situation.

Bette didn't go back to her typewriter for a long time, but there were other creative outlets. She still enjoyed modern dance. Almost immediately after the birth of her daughter she started limbering up exercises, and soon she was dancing professionally with a Washington repertory company.

Winston in the meantime was appointed to the policy planning staff of the office of the defense department. Already Lord had made a reputation for himself as a brilliant theoretician and report writer. Between 1965 and 1967 he was assigned to Geneva, Switzerland. Here he was a member of the U.S. negotiating team at the Kennedy round of tariff talks.

Bette, their daughter Lisa, and Winston departed for Switzerland together. Bette was enormously proud of her husband and was quite willing to sit on the sidelines and applaud.

But Bette Lord is an independent woman who was searching for a career of her own. Because the Swiss government does not allow foreigners to hold any job that can be handled by a Swiss native, it was hard to find something to keep her busy. Again she turned to her dancing.

She started classes for youngsters using the techniques and methods she had learned under Martha Graham. It kept her active, but still she had time on her hands. She thought of writing another book. Always her mind went back to China. She had heard many stories of her family. The one she liked best was of her maternal grandmother, who had had the courage to defy ancient custom by showing her independence. It is evident that Bette had inherited a bit of her ancestor's strength of character.

As a child her grandmother had been forced to submit to the painful practice of having her feet bound, a sign of aristocracy, so she would never be able to engage in manual labor. Even walking was a painful chore for these women who had had their feet mutilated and disfigured for the sake of a strange standard of beauty. Yet her passion for freedom led her to ride horseback and to swim in the sea, two very improper things to do in those days. The end of her grandmother's story Bette was not to learn until she returned to China. There was much she wanted to learn in the country of her birth. She kept putting off writing the stories until there might be a chance that she could return, but with the world in such a turmoil her chances seemed slim.

Winston in the meantime was to play an active role in the Vietnam peace talks. The man who picked him for the job was Henry Kissinger. Lord was present at the secret negotiations in Paris and Hanoi to end the Vietnam War. He sat in on six conferences with leaders in the Soviet Union and participated in the intricate dealings between Israel and Egypt during Kissinger's shuttle diplomacy.

In 1967 the Lords returned to Washington. Winston's job description was as a member of the international security affairs of the U.S. department of defense, a staff member of the national security council.

Back in Washington, their second child, a son named Winston Bao Lord was born. He was a beautiful child, now a handsome young man, showing the signs of his Asian heritage. Winston was a devoted parent, even taking over the task of diapering when necessary.

Bette was busy as an unofficial member of the diplomatic team keeping a busy household on track. As she is today, Bette was an efficient manager even when Winston dropped in with unexpected guests—guests whose names were often in the headlines. An invitation to the Lords was (and is) a much-prized event.

Whether entertaining or not, the Lords eat Chinese food

six nights a week. On the housekeeper's day off, hamburgers are often on the menu. Bette admits, "I used to cook and enjoy it. Now I don't cook and enjoy it."[2]

When Kissinger was made secretary of state, Lord moved from the national security council to the state department. He was known as a man who not only knew how to deliver what Mr. Kissinger wanted, but a man who was prepared to talk back.

Winston tells the story of how he learned the art of speech writing.

"One day," Lord recalls, "I gave him a speech and he said, 'Is that the best you can do?'" Lord replied that he'd try a little harder. Even after the second draft Kissinger asked, "Are you sure that's the best you can do?" After the sixth draft there was still the question, "Is this the best?" Lord answered, "Dammit, yes. I beat my brains out." Kissinger's reply was, "Okay, now I'll read it."[3]

As a surprise to both Bette and Winston, his next overseas trip was to be a special assistant on Henry Kissinger's secret trip to China. Kissinger and Lord had been sent to make arrangements for a diplomatic meeting between President Richard Nixon and the highest officials of the Chinese government. In 1971 Winston Lord and the rest of the world finally had their first glimpse of modern China. It was the first contact made with the old-line Communists of China.

Before this the United States had recognized the Nationalist government in Taiwan as representing the vast numbers of Chinese. It required delicate diplomatic maneuvers to heal the gap of hostilities that had divided China and the United States for two decades.

During the next two years Lord was the only American to accompany Henry Kissinger to all five meetings with Mao Zedong. Lord helped pave the way for normalized relations with China. Trying to break the ice during formal negotiations, Henry Kissinger arranged for Winston Lord to play a Ping-Pong match with the reigning world champion. Winston has always been a competitive athlete, but this time he was far outclassed. Ping-Pong is a major sport in China. Because of these negotiations, a team of Chinese Ping-Pong players was invited to come to the United States to demonstrate their skill. Students and diplomats would come later.

Bette wished with all her heart that she might accompany her husband, but she would be patient. Winston assured her that if the barriers for foreign visitors were relaxed she would be the first nongovernment employee to receive a visa for travel. Until that day came, he would try to make up for her disappointment by bringing her a very special present, a small vial of yellow clay from the Forbidden City in Beijing.

A 1950 photo of Bette

In 1955 Bette was graduated from high school.

A picture of Bette and Sansan taken not long after
Sansan came to the United States.

Bette and Winston Lord were married on May 4, 1963.

A photo of Bette and her daughter Lisa and
an inset of Dora holding baby Bette

Bette enjoying time with her children Lisa and Winston

The Bao family in 1982, left to right: Bette, Dora, Cathy, Sandys, and Sansan

Above: Bette and Winston with some of the embassy staff
during a Fourth of July celebration
Below left: Ambassador and Mrs. Winston Lord at the
U.S. Embassy in Beijing
Below right: Bette used sign language to welcome hearing
impaired children to the United States Embassy in Beijing
in 1987. Photo by Xinxua News Agency of China.

Above: In 1988 Bette Bao and Ambassador Winston Lord received the National Committee on U.S.-China Relations Award. Their son Winston celebrated with them.
Below: As trustee of the Freedom Forum, Bette Bao greets the president of Czechoslovakia, Vaclav Havel, in 1991.

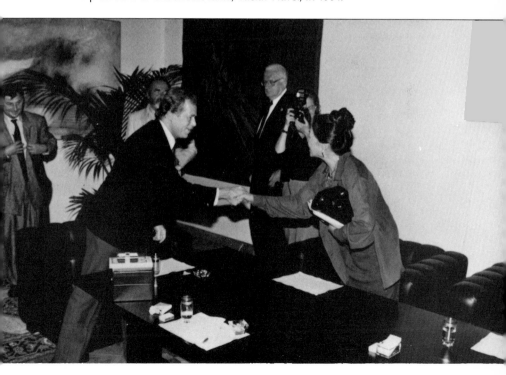

Above: Bette autographed the Chinese edition of
Spring Moon in China in 1988.
Below: Bette (center) visited her relatives in China.
Aunt Goo Ma is on the right.

Chapter 6

A HOMECOMING

In November of 1973 Bette was allowed to accompany her diplomat husband on a trip to China. Tourists still were not welcome. Letters had been sent to many of Bette's relatives hoping that a reunion might be planned. Winston would be busy with meetings. Bette would be on her own for most of the time. She was glad that she had continued to use her native language with her mother and father so that she could speak it with the same fluency she had as a child.

She was much better equipped than her husband to get along. Bette has said that she is sorry that she never taught either her husband or their two children to speak Chinese. The basic Chinese language is relatively simple — only 420 monosyllables — but depending on whether they are spoken "flat," "rising," "curling," or "falling," they have a totally different meaning. Furthermore the Chinese language does not have an alphabet, so it is necessary to learn a different ideogram for every word.

But Winston Lord always has been able to manage in diplomatic circles with an interpreter and a friendly, sincere, and trusting smile that was to serve his purposes well. It is a boyish smile that deferred to the dignity and age of others he was addressing, an important gesture in a culture that has revered age over youth.

In 1973 China was still imprisoned by the Cultural Revolution. Some of Bette's closest relatives did not dare make the effort to meet her for fear of being branded imperialists. Others avoided being alone with an American for fear that their conversations would be misconstrued as being against the Communist state.

When Bette had walked the streets in the United States she had always been aware that she was an outsider, a member of a different race. But now that she was walking the streets of China in Western clothes, she was stared at. Who was she? It was a strange feeling. She did not belong in either place completely. Yet she was able to step from one culture to the other more easily than her husband. She was able to bridge a gulf that few others understood.

Bette admitted that she often found herself hiding the unflattering side of American culture from her Chinese friends and omitting the negative pictures of Chinese life when talking to her adopted countrymen. Americans are too restless, too aggressive. Chinese revere the past, defer to their elders, and miss opportunities for progress.

When she got off the train by herself to greet her first group of relatives, she found them standing in a stiff and somber row, all carrying little red books. At first Bette thought they might be carrying the political "Bible" of the Chinese Communists, the words of Mao. Instead those little red books turned out to be dictionaries. Her relatives were afraid that they wouldn't be able to manage the language barrier. When there proved to be none, there was a much friendlier greeting.

Bette at first had planned to avoid seeing her father's sister Goo Ma because of what Sansan had told Bette. Goo Ma had been against Sansan's coming to America and had tried to put obstacles in her way. But Bette's father had been anxious that the two have a reunion. He and Goo Ma had been close when growing up, and he wasn't ready to believe that his favorite sister had had bad intentions. Bette had reluctantly agreed to a brief meeting.

Goo Ma greeted Bette warmly as if they were the closest of friends. She introduced her formally to the two officials who had been sent by the government to keep an eye on their visit. Then Goo Ma hurried Bette off before the two watchdogs could follow them. Bette at once was delighted to have met someone who was willing to scoff at authority. Goo Ma had actually snubbed not one but two officials.

When they had time together alone all of Bette's past feelings of bitterness dissolved. Goo Ma's own story was enough to bring tears and sympathy. She had been a schoolteacher once, but because of her independent thoughts she was unjustly accused of being subversive to the government. She was imprisoned with only a meager diet to sustain her. She was humiliated in front of her students by having to stand on a stage bent double with her hands raised behind her back. Her head was shaved on one side. Everything was done to break her spirit, but she survived. Those who knew her called her the Steel Woman.

Bette was to hear one horrendous story after another similar to this. No one who held any prominent position or who had had the advantage of an education was spared during the Cultural Revolution. China's history was wiped clean in the rush to install the social paradise they envisioned. It was called a political education. Those who had had the advantages of life were to take over the lowliest duties and peasants would take their "rightful" place in local authoritarian control.

Land was redistributed, but in such small parcels there was still a problem eking out a living. Religion was abolished. The state even tried to put an end to the reverence people had felt toward their ancestors. There was no room for grave sites, they were told.

Without knowing how strictly such rules had been enforced, Bette made a simple request, that she be allowed to visit the grave of her maternal grandfather. Her mother had suggested that the person to contact was her half brother Jieu Jieu. As a student Jieu Jieu had been branded a counterrevolutionary, a rightist. His friends had turned their backs. Only his father, who was a doctor, had supported him, and shared his food and room with him. When his father, Bette's grandfather, died, Jieu Jieu had collected his ashes in an urn, but with no place to bury them with honor, the ashes had been placed under his bed for more than two years.

Finally Jieu Jieu remembered a peasant whose life had been saved by Bette's grandfather. Perhaps there would be a small plot of land there for the ashes to be buried. Jieu Jieu traveled almost one hundred miles in search of the man. The former patient readily agreed to find a secret place to mark the grave of the honored doctor.

The problem came when Bette asked to be taken to the grave site of her grandfather to do him the ritual honor of sweeping his grave, a custom that had long been the practice of all families. Jieu Jieu knew that he might be implicating himself and the peasant if he admitted the rule had been broken, but in the end he decided to admit his crime. To his surprise the authorities were relieved to learn that there was really a grave for the wife of Dr. Kissinger's special assistant to sweep.

Without knowing the reason at first, Bette was kept waiting two weeks in Guangdong and Hangzhou so that a fitting gravestone could be carved and put in place for her visit.

At once Bette felt a close kinship to her uncle, who had lived through the difficult days of the past and emerged with no grudges. She wished to talk alone with this brave relative, to learn what had made him so different from others whose bitterness had tainted their lives.

One evening Bette decided to slip away from the ever-watchful official guides to walk through the streets and along the banks of the Huangpu River. She disguised herself in pigtails and a blue pajama suit that was worn by all. It was a time when Bette was almost able to slip into the mind and body of her countrymen. She walked the streets as one of them, not as the wife of a foreign official whose message was still in question.

Bette recorded her thoughts and the words of those whose lives she'd touched on tape and in meticulously detailed notes. Her visions of what she'd seen were captured on film. Again it was a happy accident that put a camera in her hands. Just as Bette was to leave for China, a friend presented the camera as a gift. An amateur, but with an artistic eye and a deep sensitive wish to record even the most mundane side of Chinese life, Bette's pictures turned out to be remarkable works of art. They were published in the *Washington Post* Sunday paper when she returned home. Someone suggested that they should be entered in a national photo contest. Much to Bette's surprise they won first place.

As a result of her trip to China in 1973 Bette signed a contract with Harper & Row to write an account of her return to China after an absence of twenty-seven years. The written record of her visit was to take longer to develop. "Becoming a novelist was not a girlhood dream," said Bette, "but a middle-age happenstance."[1]

Although President Nixon had opened negotiations with China in 1969, the political situation in the country had become most uncertain in 1974 and 1975. The government had campaigns against Confucius, the religious prophet, and Lin Piao, who had been designated Mao's political heir.

Bette was afraid that if she wrote the story of her family, whether it was good or bad, there might be repercussions for the people whose stories she would be telling. She threw out the research she had so carefully collected and decided to write a novel instead. Yet many of the stories and the setting for the action came from real life.

In 1976 the Republicans lost the national election for president of the United States. Democrat Jimmy Carter won. This meant a change of personnel in the state department as well. Cyrus Vance replaced Henry Kissinger as secretary of state, and he brought in his own staff of advisors.

Winston was relieved to have more personal time with his

family. There were no more urgent calls to pack a suitcase for an overseas flight and no more deadlines to meet. Their roles were reversed. It was Bette who now had a deadline.

A family conference was called, and it was decided to get away from the frantic pace of Washington, D.C. This couldn't have come at a better time for Bette. Writing did not come easily. It required concentration.

"Perhaps if I had known what I know now about the agony of the blank page, the imperative of endless revisions, the rigors of technique, I would never have begun a first novel."[2] But still she felt that she had something important to say about China to Western readers.

The Lords put away their city clothes. They packed up ski gear and mountain hiking boots. The hideaway they chose was Nederland, Colorado, about fifty minutes outside Boulder. Their home was perched high on a mountaintop with a breathtaking view. Civilization, which meant schools for the children, was in the valley. Every day it was Winston's job to chauffeur the kids to classes, giving Bette time to create her own make-believe world. For the next year their roles were reversed. He was the house person, she the breadwinner. He also read her manuscript many times before it went to the printer. He was a helpful and encouraging critic. It was a time when the family could be brought closer together without the rigors of life in the fast lanes of the nation's capital.

Winston Lord was able to step aside and let his wife bask in the limelight. He had been surrounded by strong women all his life. His mother was a classic example, and he expected women to excel in their chosen fields. "I spent my life being proud of being the son of Mary Lord," he has said. "My interest in international affairs was inspired by her. And now I'm proud of being the husband of Bette Lord."[3]

Winston already had had a heady taste of power in his own career. The pictures on their walls prove it. There are photographs of Winston Lord greeting Richard Nixon, another with President Gerald Ford. Here he is shaking hands with Pope John Paul II, and another where he is smiling with Zhou Enlai and Mao Zedong.

The book *Spring Moon* was six years in the writing. Bette sometimes worked from midnight until 5:00 A.M. six days a week, so she wouldn't miss the family's schedule. Bette admits to being a night owl naturally, and this was the only time that absolute quiet was guaranteed.

When asked if the children were a help in any way, Bette laughs. They always knew when she was working because she would shut herself up in her little room. When she was interrupted she had a terrible temper. The children had no idea that their mother was about to become a very famous author. The advance publicity was out, and the advance payment of $500,000 demonstrated that the publisher was confident the book was going to be a blockbuster.

The novel was published in eleven different languages, and without permission by a company in Taiwan who was not a party to any international copyright laws. Bette was shocked and angry when she read the unauthorized version. She felt that they had completely distorted her work, reinterpreting certain phrases and twisting meanings. Other sections had been entirely deleted. "He [the translator] has mutilated my characters and my philosophical outlook."[4]

Back in the United States reviews carried extravagant praise. Ronald Nevans said in the *Saturday Review* that the book was "one of the most remarkable novels ever to explain the East to the West."

Not only had Bette written a suspenseful narrative about five generations of the Chang family, she had covered a hundred years of history. The novel shows the contrast between the character Spring Moon, who remains true to her Confucian ideals, and Lustrous Jade, her daughter, who becomes a Communist revolutionary. The book appeared on *The New York Times* best-seller list for thirty weeks.

Bette became an instant celebrity. The Lord family returned from their chosen isolation to New York City. Immediately following publication of the book, Bette was away from home on a series of promotional tours where she could meet her reading public and sign autographs. Some successful writers are tongue-tied at the podium, but not Bette. She is an excellent public speaker and an interesting one at that.

There is an inner glow that sets Bette apart, a style of self-assurance and beauty that mesmerizes an audience of one or hundreds. She often dresses in the Eastern manner with clothes made for her in Hong Kong. Usually she sweeps her hair up in a crown atop her head. But there's the Bette Lord in jeans and T-shirt, thigh-length hair cascading down her back, eating hamburgers, and relaxing with her family.

Bette is ambitious. Her goals are set to exceed what has gone before. But she admits that the course of her life has already surpassed her dreams. Even as a novelist, she could not have plotted such a favorable fate. At times it is frightening, she admits. Can it all last?

Again the American swing in politics was to cause a major reshuffling of personnel in the state department. On January 20, 1980 Ronald Reagan, a Republican, was elected president of the United States. It also was the day the American hostages, who had been held captive by Iran, were released.

For a time the American public put faraway China out of its mind, but again Henry Kissinger was back working for the government, although not as secretary of state. Since 1977 others had taken over that job. Kissinger was now made head of a federal commission set up to develop foreign policy with Central America. Quite naturally he solicited Winston

Lord's help. Lord was named senior counselor of the president's bipartisan committee on Central America from 1983 to 1984. The Lords now commuted between Washington, D.C., and a luxurious New York Park Avenue apartment.

With time on her hands, Bette was again thinking of writing. With two popular books to her credit, publishers were clamoring for more, maybe a story of her own life in contrast to Sansan's. Bette still felt more comfortable telling it from another point of view.

The Year of the Boar and Jackie Robinson is a wonderful, warm, and often humorous look at the trials of a young Chinese girl growing up in Brooklyn. The charming, sentimental, amusing story of Shirley Temple Wong is really the tale of Bette Bao when she first arrived in this country. It was written for children, but is enjoyed by every age. It tells of Shirley's struggles to become Americanized at a time in her life when it was very important to adopt all the popular myths of American culture. She becomes an expert at rattling off baseball statistics and thanks to a very influential classmate, even tries out for the local game of stickball.

Bette gives a warm and touching picture of how an outsider struggles to be one of the group. It is a must on the reading list for all who have ever shunned someone because of a different ethnic background. Again the book was a great success. Bette had finally found a career for herself.

Chapter 7

AN AMBASSADOR'S WIFE

It was at this time that Arthur W. Hummel, Jr., was retiring as the ambassador to the People's Republic of China. Winston Lord was almost everyone's choice to fill the job. His credentials were superb. He had been present during the very first Western contact with the country. At the American Foreign Service Association, the union that represents state department employees, Mr. Lord was regarded as a political appointee of the highest order.

During his early visits to China, he and Bette had become enthusiastic supporters of Deng Xiaoping and his reforms. They recognized that while the people of China were not heading directly toward democratic reform, they were heading for economic stability. In comparison with the other giant Communist country, the Soviet Union, China was able to feed its people. There were goods in the marketplace. With patience, political reforms would come later, they hoped.

Bette had strongly advised some of the people she had met on her earlier visits to China not to abandon their political influence by dropping out of party politics. She was sure change could come from within the Communist party.

Some conservatives who held opposing views tried to block Winston Lord's appointment as ambassador to China. As an aide to Henry Kissinger during the Nixon era, Lord had helped normalize relations with China, opening up dialogue for exchange of trade. There were those who disagreed. Lord also was associated with two organizations conservatives loved to hate. He was president of the Council on Foreign Relations and a member of the Trilateral Commission, a private group that advocates economic and political cooperation between Western allies. David Rockefeller had donated $250,000 to a Winston Lord fund set up by the Council on Foreign Relations to strengthen the group's study of Asian affairs. Again this was used as proof that Lord would be too lenient in his dealings with the Chinese government, that he would put their needs ahead of the concerns of the United States.

During several months of hearings Bette tried desperately not to think too much about the confirmation, but there was no mistaking the tension both she and Winston were experiencing. There was a long, sometimes grueling, aggravating wait before the legislative branch of the government could set the wheels in motion for the final confirmation.

There were six months of security checks and three-and-a-half months while the government went over Winston Lord's financial records to make sure there were no conflicts of interest. Then six weeks after a hearing before the Senate Foreign Relations Subcommittee had cleared his name for final passage, Senator Jesse Helms made his bid to hold the appointment in limbo while he asked more questions with the express purpose of blocking anyone who did not subscribe to his bedrock anti-Communist views. He was against any support of a government that did not measure up to his ideas of political conservatism. Helms was very concerned about abortion in China. Because Winston did not say he disapproved of China's abortion policy, Helms objected to Winston's appointment.

China had stepped up a population control system. Families were supposed to have only one child. Frequently this meant supporting abortions. With no logical reason for attacking Lord's credentials, Helms kept hammering away at his ethical views on abortion policies. Lord diplomatically replied that he would take his guidance from the president.

It was important that the post of ambassador to China be filled as soon as possible. If left vacant, it would be considered a breach in diplomatic procedure. The Chinese were sure to feel they were being discriminated against.

Finally President Reagan intervened to break the impasse, and the Lords were ready to pack their bags for an extended stay in China. It was a dream come true for Bette.

In her book *Legacies*, Bette states that, "Although Winston was the one who had taken the oath of office, I vowed on that first night to be worthy of the honor of representing my adopted country—the honor that he had earned but that I shared simply because I had said yes in answer to the fateful question my Anglo-Saxon classmate had popped twenty-three years before."[1]

It was as if fate had had a hand in all the events of her life up to that time, a fatalism grounded in the culture of her country.

Their stay in China had come at an especially important time in history. Mao's brand of communism was being supplanted by the policies of Deng Xiaoping. Much was happening in China during the middle 1980s that would have been unthinkable a few years before. With its long, illustrious history, China is so rooted in its past that it would take patience to see a radical change, but the Lords would be there to help steer that future. So much interaction had been cut off by the Chinese revolution because China had wanted Western technology but had worked hard to keep out Western ideas. Now there was someone who understood their problems and in a tactful way could bring about change.

The Lords arrived in Beijing on a cold, clear November night and were driven to the official residence at 17 Guang

Hua Lu. Bette remembers being curious about the noise she heard, a thumping on the fender of the car. It was caused by the flapping of the American flag attached to the fender. The flag signified the official limousine reserved only for the ambassador. It was a heady, but unnerving, feeling that surely this time she must follow her mother's advice when she was entering the fifth grade in Brooklyn. She really was an ambassador, at least close to one, who would be representing her adopted country. It was a responsibility she took very seriously. No one could have worked harder at her job. Other wives in the diplomatic service have been relieved of their hostess duties, but in China this would be one of the most important duties, to win over the friendship and trust of a people who were grounded in suspicion.

Although it was Winston who had taken the oath to represent the United States to the best of his ability, Bette was very much involved in the work as immediate advisor to her husband, interpreting even the casual approach to meeting people. Hers was an unofficial title, of course, but the very fact that she could converse fluently in the Chinese language opened up many channels that might otherwise have remained blocked. Although Winston had the uncanny ability to make friends and earn trust through his limited snippets of pidgin Mandarin, there would always be a gulf of intimacy. The fact that he had chosen a Chinese woman for his wife gave him an added edge of respect. Too many white foreigners had looked down on the Chinese in past history. This was ample proof that Ambassador Lord held no such hostile feelings.

Moving into ambassadorial quarters might seem glamorous at first, but Bette was well aware of the drawbacks from the very beginning. The property is actually held in trust, with the ambassadorial staff acting as guardian. There would be no chance to knock out a few walls and completely redecorate as she wished. Certainly ambassadors have an obligation to keep government property in up-to-date condition, but changing decor every few years is definitely not practical.

The formality of the reception room was a challenge to the Lord's sense of warm congeniality. The den was often called the Fourth of July Room because it was seldom used except on that day. While lesser dignitaries were served in the gardens of the embassy compound, more important officials were seated and served food in the den. Bette and Winston disapproved of such class distinctions in what the Communists called their classless society, but it was a tradition that was next to impossible to break. Those who expected this special attention would have been angered if asked to mingle with the masses.

Even the practice of hiring help was not left up to the discretion of the Lords. Every one of the 250 local people who worked for the embassy as janitors, drivers, laborers, mail carriers, telephone operators, research assistants, and cooks were assigned to the Lords by the Diplomatic Services Bureau of the People's Republic of China. If one turned out to be incompetent, the Lords either had to put up with the bungled service or do without.

Bette's experience with the kitchen staff would have tried the patience of the most diplomatic employer. During their first year it was most important to open the doors of the embassy to frequent social functions. To cope with such a schedule Bette had to put up with a series of head cooks. The first was efficient, frugal, and able to cook for huge numbers with no complaints. But as soon as he had settled into the routine, he was reassigned to the Chinese Embassy in Moscow.

The second chef was a temperamental dictator in the kitchen. He soon had the entire staff in a nervous series of confrontations. He served such excellent meals that Bette was prepared to put up with fits of temperament for the sake of embassy guests, who were extremely impressed with the results from the kitchen. However, after only a short tour of duty he resigned, due to high blood pressure he said, explaining that a fortune-teller had predicted his death in the near future. He did not want to ruin the reputation of Mrs. Lord by dying at his post as if she had been working him to death.

The third replacement was inexperienced, unskilled, and seemingly unable to follow orders. One of the most complicated kitchen disasters, Bette Lord explains in her book *Legacies*. For Thanksgiving dinner more than a hundred guests had been invited to share a typical American dinner of roast turkey. The chef admitted that he had seen a turkey only once before in a zoo, but with explicit directions, preparations seemed to be progressing more smoothly than could have been expected. Bette toured the kitchen to make sure that all was in readiness. The six birds seemed to be turning a golden brown right on schedule.

While making her inspection, Bette happened to see a large box near the stove. Bette asked what was in it. The answer was onions from America. Onions definitely would not have been ordered from America. They were available for pennies in all local markets. When Bette peered inside the box she saw a half-empty box of bulbs. It suddenly came to her that these must be the hyacinth bulbs sent to her by a friend who was an avid gardener.

Had any been used? Yes, they were now seasoning the stuffing of the turkey. The question was, could they be poisonous? Bette first tried to call a medical center and could reach no one. Finally after a frantic call to the Poison Control Center in Atlanta, Georgia, the answer came back that the meal would be safe. How it would taste was another question. No one seemed to complain that day, but there were fewer spring flowers in the embassy garden than had been planned.

One way to encourage dialogue between the two countries was to invite as many people as their busy schedule would permit to the embassy for talks. Bette Bao Lord transformed their residence into a place where Chinese artists and writers could meet and talk about the events that were daily changing the oppressive atmosphere laid on the country by Mao.

Bette's sincere concern for others led many to unburden themselves with much more freedom than ever before. Of course with this came the requests for favors. Could Bette please see that property once belonging to a family be returned to them? Could Ambassador Lord secure visas and entry into the United States, or scholarships? Bette had to explain that her position as wife of the American ambassador did not allow her to grant such requests, and neither could her husband become involved in internal affairs.

Chinese business had become an elaborate exchange of favors, something that had been slowing down the rate of progress. For example, someone goes in to buy a television and is told there are none available. Then someone else walks in who knows the salesman and can buy one, because of past "courtesies." All business seemed to be done by an exchange of favors, rather than by following rules. If you were a party member you had influence. This caused smoldering discontent.

Traditionally the Chinese have felt the need to conform to the Confucian standard of behavior, to defer to a person older or more important than oneself. On top of that there is a rigid Communist system that demands yet more conformity. This has held back China's development. Those individuals who wanted to break with tradition and set new rules were considered traitors to their country.

Bette has tried to explain some very important differences between the two cultures. Individuality is not prized. In China some 95 percent of the people are of the same ethnic group, while in America many countries of origin are represented. In China people are classified more by their educational background—peasants and intellectuals. Chinese, unlike Americans, are wary of making new friends. Old ones are safe, new ones can be risky.

Bette and Winston tried to invite a broad range of nationals to come forth and be welcomed by the embassy staff. A wide assortment of entertainment was provided. For the more Westernized diplomats, there was disco dancing, and no two could have been better performers than Bette and Winston.

Chinese of all classes seem to have been fascinated with American films whenever they were available. Bette did the next best thing, she brought Hollywood to them, almost. A production of *The Caine Mutiny* was performed by the top theatrical group in China, the People's Art Theater—with Charlton Heston in person as their director.

Bette tried to show off the best in American culture—from

jazz groups and country singers performing live in the garden, to plays and opera performances. Anyone who was passing through China got an invitation to perform at the embassy for the Chinese people.

On the tenth anniversary of the day when diplomatic channels were reopened between the United States and China, the embassy was open for a huge reception. A multimedia show in which slides and live performances were interwoven for some three to five thousand people gave the Chinese a better look at their new friend America. One of the "minor" feats of the day was the preparation of thirty-six thousand Chinese dumplings for the hungry crowd. Bette herself supervised the event, which was to be the talk of Beijing for days to come.

Bette also was able to arrange more visits with her relatives. This time they were begging for invitations. In 1986 Bette's mother and father returned to their homeland after an absence of forty years. It was a time for rejoicing and of course an excuse for a reunion party. The invitation list was restricted to sixty, just those who were living in Beijing, Tianjin, and Xian. Bette's father acted as master of ceremonies and kept his audience entertained with bits of early memories.

Before the guests were to leave it had been arranged that a group picture be taken. As Bette describes in her book

Legacies there was a mad dash to get front-row seats. Winston naturally, in his informal way, sat on the floor beside Bette. There was nervous laughter, then nods of approval. Winston had showed tact in knowing enough to take his rightful humble place, in spite of his exalted official position. Again with a warm grin and a friendly smile, he had bridged the cultural gap and made friends without saying many words.

In the fall of 1988 a second reunion was planned to coincide with Bette's parents' golden-wedding anniversary and Bette and Winston's silver anniversary. There was poetry reading, the performance of Chinese opera, and fireworks. But the next anniversary would be celebrated in the United States. Winston Lord felt that he had established a firm support for friendly negotiations in trade, in reciprocal educational opportunities, and in the difficult ambivalence between Taiwan and Beijing. It was time to move on to other pursuits.

Bette supported the move. She was particularly sensitive to the fact that some people might consider her activities purely social trimmings. This was far from the truth. Although she had to entertain or go to banquets a dozen times a week, these activities had opened the doors for serious international dialogues that had not been possible before.

Instead, she would have much preferred sitting at her typewriter transcribing some of the heartfelt stories she had been privileged to hear. Her discretion was trusted. People had opened themselves to her with a frankness they had denied others. They could both feel it was a job well done.

In 1989 student demonstrators in Tiananmen Square
erected a replica of the Statue of Liberty that they called
"The Goddess of Democracy."

Chapter 8

TELLING THE STORY OF CHINA

On April 15, 1989 it was time for Bette and Winston to say good-bye to their friends at the embassy. It was also the day Hu Yaobang died. He had been the former party general secretary. But two years earlier he had been removed from his post by Deng Xiaoping at the urging of the conservatives. Hu Yaobang's death gave the progressive body of college students a reason to mourn and to parade their grievances in public. They made Hu Yaobang their hero. Students on the Beijing campuses wore black armbands and erected posters in honor of Hu Yaobang, posters also calling for democratic reforms.

It was unfortunate that Winston and Bette Lord would be leaving at this critical time of political unrest, but plans had been made months before. Bette was to leave with Winston for a three-day stopover in Hong Kong. She would then be exchanging her diplomatic passport for a regular citizen's travel permit and returning to Beijing for a short stay. She would be acting as interpreter and consultant for the CBS television crew who had come to China's capital to report on the visit of the Soviet leader Mikhail Gorbachev.

There were many others who could translate the language, but Bette had been asked to stay behind because of her intimate knowledge of Chinese customs and her wide circle of friends within the country. She would be invaluable in reporting the political sentiments of a cross section of the population.

When Bette returned from Hong Kong, the student movement had already gotten underway. There were signs and placards everywhere. The streets were filling with students who had taken time from classes to hold meetings to discuss programs of reform they hoped the government would at least be willing to debate.

Bette immediately sensed a different spirit in the air. In the past people's spirits had been low. Change had been promised, but party officials were languishing in luxury, pretending to meet the concerns of the masses, ignoring the blatant corruption within their ranks. People had felt powerless to change the system. Now the young were leading the way from group thinking to speaking out.

By April 22 tens of thousands of students who had marched on Tiananmen Square defied police orders to leave. While memorial services were being held for Hu Yaobang at the Great Hall of the People, the students gathered to pay their respects in Tiananmen.

Four days later the official *People's Daily* published an editorial accusing the student movement of being unpatriotic. It accused the movement of a planned conspiracy to cause chaos with ulterior motives of overthrowing the government.

In truth the students wished to work within the system, seeking gradual reform within the Communist party, promoting the very goals the party had proclaimed. They petitioned only for rights set forth in the Communist constitution. At the beginning no one attacked the leadership or called for Western-style democracy. The students' platform boiled down to two requests; acknowledgment that the demonstrators were patriotic and that there would be no punishment for speaking out, and, second, that arrangements would be set up for talks between political leaders and elected student leaders.

Deng Xiaoping and his comrades, most in their mid-eighties, had been in power too long. They had lost touch with the sentiments of the people. If they had shown at least some compromise at this time, bloodshed could have been averted, Bette felt.

She watched helplessly. All she could do was to relay the sentiments of the people of China to the listening world. Her office had been set up in the Shangri-La Hotel. Her job was to assist reporters when they needed more information from around the country.

Bette relied on her friends in supplying the news. They kept her posted on what was happening in their own neighborhoods, but eventually Bette began calling hotels, hospitals, police stations—anywhere telephone operators were on duty twenty-four hours a day. She was in contact with almost three hundred cities throughout China. There was a new sense of cooperation. People were glad to talk to her and help her.

As Bette says in her book *Legacies*, "People who had traditionally looked to others to liberate them had now liberated themselves....It united them....For the first time in their history Chinese were caring for strangers."[1]

When Bette was not attending the bank of telephones in front of her, she took time out to walk the streets to see for herself what was happening. Even middle-school students were helping to set up road blocks. A group of blind people had made their way to Beijing. "When the convoys come, we will lay our bodies in their path,"[2] they said.

People from all walks of life offered their help. Some donated money, food, and clothing. Homemade signs were everywhere. "Kind people, protect our students."[3]

On May 3 the government appealed for calm. Reportedly the state council was willing to respond to some of the students' demands, but they would not state what action would be taken. The following day more than 250,000 demonstrators marched on the square to celebrate the seventieth anniversary of China's first student movement. As Bette explains, "In

Chinese history, students are seen as the conscience of society."[4]

More than a thousand Chinese journalists delivered a petition to the government calling for freedom of the press. Their banners read: "We refuse to lie anymore."

On May 13 when there was no response to their moderate demands, two thousand students launched a hunger strike in Tiananmen Square to protest the April 26 editorial. On the fourth day of the hunger strike over two hundred strikers were hospitalized from dehydration, sunstroke, and exposure. People all over the country felt sympathy for the brave ones who were putting their lives on the line.

In the meantime Gorbachev and the Chinese leaders were meeting in the Great Hall. The leaders were more interested, it would seem, in international trade policies than in what was happening in their own country. Sentiment was running high, not only in the nation's capital but throughout the provinces. For seven weeks there were peaceful demonstrations in almost three hundred cities throughout China.

Finally on May 17 Party General Secretary Zhao Ziyang appealed to the students to return to their campuses, but his statement did not reverse the April 26 editorial, making the leaders of the movement liable for court action and prison. Twice Ziyang visited with the hunger strikers. Feeling that their primary goals had been met and that meetings had been promised, they agreed to end their strike. But at the same time Premier Li Peng announced martial law and ordered troops to move in and clear the square.

On May 23 three men with no connection to the student movement threw paint on the portrait of Mao Zedong that hangs on the Gate of Heavenly Peace in Tiananmen Square. Students captured the vandals so there was no need to punish innocent protestors.

By May 30, 1989 most of the students had evacuated the square. Only two thousand or three thousand were left and they were mostly from outside Beijing waiting for a way to get home. Those remaining unveiled a plaster statue they called the "Goddess of Democracy." It bore a striking resemblance to the pose of the Statue of Liberty in the U.S.

It had been two weeks since the Gorbachev visit. Most of the CBS crew had left. Bette too prepared to leave, thinking that bloodshed had been averted. Although not all the student's aims had been resolved, she felt there was hope if the government would only agree to talks with the disaffected citizens who had so long been patiently waiting for reform. To have the grievances made so public ought to have warned officials that reforms were necessary. She had no illusions about the difficult days ahead, but she was hopeful that the China Spring, as it was being called, the fresh spirit of hope, would flourish and bear fruit.

Bette was home in New York City by the weekend of June 3

to 5 when the massacre occurred. Tens of thousands of troops advanced on Beijing. At first they were held back by the citizens' barricades, but later with reinforcements they crashed their way to the square. They opened fire, and hundreds of people were killed and wounded. No one knows the exact figure. With the government in control, censorship kept the outside world from knowing the true extent of the killing.

Bette was horrified at the pictures that were smuggled out of the country. She feels that if only a few concessions had been made to the student movement, China could have continued its march toward reforms in an orderly manner. Now world opinion has brought on *the big chill*, a condemnation of China's actions by cutting off all but the most elemental bridges of diplomacy. Many in the American government feel that the U.S. should turn its back on China and have no dealings with China at all.

Bette Lord and her husband have spoken out in asking the world not to condemn the Chinese people for the atrocities committed by a few. They say the free world should be willing to stretch a hand of friendship toward those who may some day be in the role of leaders. There should be hope for intellectuals who may one day have the opportunity to speak out again.

Bette does not believe the students died in vain. The massacre broke the spell that Deng Xiaoping had upon the people. "After a change of heart comes a change of mind and then a change of system."[5]

Bette's book *Legacies: A Chinese Mosaic* was already in progress in the spring of 1989, but suddenly world events made it all the more important for publication to be immediate. The book was written from information she had gathered from many interviews and other recordings given her upon her departure from China. These were personal stories of a variety of contemporary Chinese, who tell of their persecutions and their friends' persecutions, expressed candidly for the first time. Bette Lord writes she has included "the most costly gifts any Chinese could give, the most precious gifts a writer could receive...the uncensored stories of their lives."[6] To relieve the somberness she has added some of her own tales about her family and her role as wife of the American ambassador.

Again her work was included in *The New York Times* bestseller list and the book has been translated into ten languages.

The reviews were enthusiastic. Ruth Price wrote for the *Chicago Tribune* book section, "With remarkable subtlety and precision [Lord] captures the ambivalence and contradictions that characterize Chinese history and its people...Lord has done a splendid job...of reducing the unwieldy package of Chinese history to a human scale and bringing forward the tragedy of individual lives with a novelist's grace and eloquence."

With Bette's next book she has again turned to fiction. The title is *The Middle Heart*, but she is still working on the manuscript. She admits, "I'm still the insecure person that dreads the blank piece of paper. I love having written. I hate the process of writing."[7]

Bette and her husband are both writers with their offices just twenty feet apart in their New York apartment. They have a multitude of friends and are both much sought after as lecturers. Bette is a member of The Freedom Forum, a group that fosters the exchange of ideas, research, and cultures throughout the world. As a writer, it is easier for her to get her message across to a broader audience than if she wrote as a political scientist. Both Lords speak in favor of furthering Chinese-American relations.

Their two children are college graduates seeking careers on opposite coasts. Lisa, an aspiring actress, lives in California. Young Winston, a recent graduate of Yale, works in Washington. Sister Sansan also works in Washington. Cathy is married to an artist, Bennett Bean, a well-known potter. She is a teacher of philosophy at Mount Clair College. It is obvious that Dora and Sandys Bao have instilled respect for scholarship and the arts in their three talented daughters. Family ties are very close.

It has been said "Chinese cannot outrun the shadows of their ancestors."[8] Bette has never tried.

Bette taped a series called "The Heart of the Dragon"
for public television in 1985. She is standing with newsman
Jim Lehrer holding a Chinese dragon.

NOTES

Chapter 2
1. Ken Adelman, "Out of China," *The Washingtonian* (August 1990): 32.
2. Enid Nemy, "Combines Two Cultures," *The New York Times* (August 30, 1981).

Chapter 3
1. Ken Adelman, "Out of China," *The Washingtonian* (August 1990): 32.
2. Bette Bao Lord, *Legacies: A Chinese Mosaic* (New York: Alfred A. Knopf, 1990): 217.
3. Kristin McMurran, "Winston Lord May Be an Old China Hand But Wife Bette Wrote the Book on Mandarins," *People* (November 23, 1981): 90.
4. Ibid., 93.
5. Lord, *Legacies: A Chinese Mosaic*, 12.

Chapter 4
1. Lord, Bette, *Eighth Moon by Sansan as told to Bette Lord* (New York: Harper & Row, Publishers, Incorporated, 1964): 213.

Chapter 5
1. "Henry's Little Kissingers," *Newsweek* (December 10, 1973): 62.
2. Enid Nemy, "Combines Two Cultures," *The New York Times* (August 30, 1981).
3. Kristin McMurran, "Winston Lord

May Be an Old China Hand But Wife Bette Wrote the Book on Mandarins," *People* (November 23, 1981): 90.

Chapter 6
1. *Contemporary Authors* (Detroit: Gale Research, 1983): Volume 107: 297.
2. Ibid.
3. Enid Nemy, "Combines Two Cultures," *The New York Times* (August 30, 1981).
4. *Contemporary Authors*, 297.

Chapter 7
1. Bette Bao Lord, *Legacies: A Chinese Mosaic* (New York: Alfred A. Knopf, 1990): 14.

Chapter 8
1. Bette Bao Lord, *Legacies: A Chinese Mosaic* (New York: Alfred A. Knopf, 1990): 190.
2. Ibid., 189.
3. Ibid.
4. Ken Adelman, "Out of China," *The Washingtonian* (August 1990): 34.
5. Ibid., 36.
6. Bette Bao Lord, *Legacies: A Chinese Mosaic*, 15.
7. *Contemporary Authors* (Detroit: Gale Research, 1983): Volume 107.
8. Bette Bao Lord, *Legacies: A Chinese Mosaic*, 6.

BETTE BAO LORD 1938–

1938 Betty Bao Lord is born in Shanghai, China. Japanese take over city of Canton, China. Pearl S. Buck receives Nobel prize for literature.

1939 Japanese occupy island of Hainan. Francisco Franco becomes dictator of Spain. Germany invades Poland; World War II begins (ends 1945). Igor Sikorsky (a Russian-American) constructs the first helicopter.

1940 France is occupied by Germany. Franklin D. Roosevelt is elected U.S. president for the third time. A puppet government is established in China.

1941 Germany invades the former Soviet Union. Japanese bomb U.S. military base at Pearl Harbor; U.S. and Great Britain declare war on Japan.

1942 "Manhattan Project" of intensive atomic research begins in the U.S. Physicist Enrico Fermi (an Italian-American) splits the atom.

1943 General Chiang Kai-shek is sworn in as chairman of the national government; Chiang, President Roosevelt, and Great Britain's prime minister Winston Churchill confer in Cairo, Egypt.

1944 Roosevelt is elected U.S. president for the fourth time.

1945 The first atomic bomb is detonated near Alamogordo, New Mexico. U.S. drops first atomic bombs on Hiroshima and Nagasaki, Japan; Adolf Hitler commits suicide; Benito Mussolini of Italy is killed; Germany and Japan surrender to Allies; World War II ends. China regains control of Manchuria and Taiwan. Arab League is founded to oppose the creation of Jewish state of Israel. The United Nations is established.

1946 Sandys Bao, Bette Bao's father, comes to the United States to work for the Nationalist government of China; Bette, her sister, and their mother Dora join Sandys Bao later in the year. United States grants independence to the Philippines. Winston Churchill of Great Britain gives "Iron Curtain" speech. United Nations General Assembly holds its first session in London.

1947 India and Pakistan become independent. Scientists invent the transistor at the Bell Laboratories. U.S. Secretary of State George Marshall proposes the European Recovery Program, also called the Marshall Plan.

1948 Mahatma Gandhi is assassinated in India (born 1869). Chiang Kai-shek is elected president of Republic of China by the National Assembly under the newly adopted constitution. T.S. Eliot receives Nobel prize for literature.

1949 The Chinese Communists win a total victory in China. People's Republic of China is proclaimed with Mao Zedong as Chinese Communist Party (CCP) leader— chairman; the Bao family decides to stay in U.S. and not to return to China. The Red Guards, a national organization of teenagers, is formed in China; possession of firearms becomes illegal in China. Eleven Communists in the U.S. are convicted of conspiracy to overthrow the government.

1950 United Kingdom recognizes Israel. Korean War begins (ends 1953). U.S. agrees to send arms and troops to Korea to fight the North Koreans. A thirty-year Chinese-Soviet Treaty is signed.

1951 First electronic computer for commercial purpose is installed at the U.S. Census Bureau. U.S. Congress passes Twenty-second Amendment, setting two terms (eight years) as the maximum service for president. Color television is introduced in the U.S.

1952 Richard M. Nixon is elected vice-president of the United States. King George VI of England dies; his daughter, Elizabeth II, becomes Queen. The first hydrogen bomb is exploded at Eniwetok Atoll in the Pacific Ocean.

1953 As a result of cease-fire agreement, Korea is divided along 38th parallel into North and South Korea. China institutes its first Five-Year Plan to promote industrialization. Joseph Stalin of the U.S.S.R. dies. Nikita Khrushchev becomes head of Soviet Communist Party Central Committee.

1954 United States signs a mutual defense pact with Nationalist China. Communists in Vietnam take Dien Bien Phu and occupy Hanoi. First (annual) Jazz Festival is held at Newport, Rhode Island.

1955 China begins agricultural collectivization by organizing farmers into agricultural cooperatives. U.S. begins sending aid to Vietnam. Dictator Juan Perón of Argentina is overthrown.

1956 Hungarians revolt against Soviet occupation of their country; Soviet troops invade Hungary. Israeli army invades Sinai Peninsula and British and French troops occupy the Suez. Pakistan declares itself an Islamic country. Gamal Abdul Nassar becomes president of Egypt.

1957 Many Chinese dissidents are sent for reeducation in labor camps in what is called the anti-rightist campaign; government seizes small family plots. Andrei Gromyko becomes Soviet foreign minister. Soviets launch first man-made satellites, *Sputnik I* and *II*, to circle the earth. European Common Market is established.

1958 China begins the Great Leap Forward (1958-60); emphasis is placed on the rapid development of labor-intensive industries. U.S. launches its first satellite. Alaska becomes forty-ninth state of the U.S. Charles de Gaulle becomes president of France. U.S. establishes National Aeronautics and Space Administration (NASA). Boris Pasternak publishes *Dr. Zhivago.*

1959 Bette graduates from Tufts University; Winston Lord, Bette's husband, graduates from Yale University. Among widespread violence and rebellion against Chinese rule, Dalai Lama — the Tibetan spiritual leader — takes exile in India. Hawaii becomes fiftieth U.S. state. Fidel Castro overthrows Cuban dictator Batista and becomes president.

1960 Bette and Winston receive master's degrees from Fletcher School of Law and Diplomacy. Bette moves to Hawaii and becomes assistant director at East-West Cultural Center at University of Hawaii (resigns in 1961). Soviet Union withdraws its technical help from China; Chinese government returns small family plots to people. Nixon and John F. Kennedy hold first television debates between presidential candidates; Kennedy defeats Nixon in presidential election. Leonid Brezhnev becomes president of the U.S.S.R.

1961 Bette becomes program officer at Fulbright Exchange Program (resigns in 1963). U.S. breaks diplomatic ties with Cuba. Berlin Wall is erected.

1962 Sansan Bao, Bette's youngest sister, escapes from China and is reunited with her family in the United States. A serious Cold War crisis is avoided when Soviet Union agrees to remove missiles from Cuba. U.S. establishes military advisors in South Vietnam. John Steinbeck receives Nobel prize for literature. William Faulkner dies (born 1897).

1963 Winston Lord and Bette Bao are married in May. President Kennedy is assassinated in Dallas; Lyndon B. Johnson becomes president of the United States. Rev. Martin Luther King, Jr. is arrested in Birmingham, Alabama.

1964 Bette becomes a naturalized citizen of the United States. Elizabeth Pillsbury Lord, Bette and Winston's first child, is born; Bette publishes (with her sister Sansan) *Eighth Moon: The True Story of a Young Girl's Life in Communist China*; it is later translated into fifteen languages. IBM produces the Magnetic Tape/Selectric Typewriter. China becomes the fifth nation to explode a nuclear bomb. Vietnam War escalates. Alexei Kosygin becomes prime minister and Leonid Brezhnev becomes Communist party secretary in U.S.S.R. Martin Luther King, Jr. receives Nobel Peace Prize.

1965 Winston Lord is assigned a post in Geneva, Switzerland; Bette teaches and performs modern dance in Geneva. Electronic calculator is introduced. U.S.S.R. supplies arms to North Vietnam. Anti-war demonstrations sweep U.S. Great Britain celebrates 750th anniversary of Magna Carta. Great Proletarian Cultural Revolution starts (finishes 1969).

1966 All Chinese schools and universities are closed to allow students to participate in the Cultural Revolution; more and more students participate in the Red Guards groups. One million people demonstrate in the Tiananmen Square. President Lyndon B. Johnson of U.S. tours the Far East. British Guiana becomes the independent nation of Guyana.

1967 Lords return to the United States from Switzerland. Bette's second child, Winston Bao Lord, is born. Arab nations and Israel engage in Six-Day War; Israel defeats Arab nations. U.S. bombs Hanoi, North Vietnam. Chinese Embassy personnel are attacked in Moscow. China detonates its first hydrogen bomb.

1968 Soviet Union invades and occupies Czechoslovakia. Nixon is elected president. Paris Peace Talks on Vietnam begins. Albania withdraws from the Warsaw Pact. Martin Luther King, Jr. is shot in Memphis. *Apollo 8* of U.S. becomes the first spacecraft to orbit the moon.

1969 China declares the Soviet Union its principal enemy. Neil Armstrong of U.S. is the first man to walk on the moon. Ho Chi-Minh, president of the Democratic Republic of Vietnam, dies. China carries out first successful underground nuclear test.

1970 Bette becomes conference director for National Conference for the Associated Councils of the Arts (resigns in 1971). After the coup in Cambodia, Prince Norodom Sihanouk establishes a government in exile in Beijing. China launches an earth-orbiting satellite. U.S. invades Cambodia. China establishes diplomatic relations with Canada and Italy. *Apollo 13* is launched from Cape Kennedy. Soviet novelist Alexander Solzhenitsyn receives the Nobel prize for literature.

1971 Henry A. Kissinger, U.S. National Security Adviser, makes a secret trip to China; Winston Lord accompanies him. People's Republic of China is admitted in the United Nations; Taiwan loses its UN membership. American table-tennis team visits China. Chairman Mao invites President Nixon to China; Winston Lord accompanies Kissinger to China. Women are granted right to vote in Switzerland. Cigarette advertisements are banned from U.S. television.

1972 President Nixon meets with Mao Zedong in Beijing; Winston Lord is part of these meetings. Twenty countries (including Japan and West Germany) establish diplomatic relations with China. Bangladesh (formerly East Pakistan) becomes an independent nation; China vetoes Bangladesh membership in the United Nations.

Nixon is reelected president; he is the first U.S. president to visit China and the Soviet Union. U.S. reestablishes diplomatic ties with China.

1973 U.S. and China exchange liaison offices (quasi-embassy). Bette is allowed to go to China with her diplomat husband; she meets most of her relatives. Cease-fire is declared in Vietnam. Middle East unrest causes oil prices to double, creating world-wide energy crisis.

1974 Bette is awarded National Graphics Arts Prize for her photographic essay on China. Nixon resigns as president. Arabs lift oil embargo to the West. Charles A. Lindbergh, aviation pioneer, dies (born 1902). India becomes the sixth nation to explode a nuclear device.

1975 Xerox corporation releases its computerized typing system with their Diablo printer. Chiang Kai-shek dies and is succeeded by his son, Chiang Ching-Kuo, as chairman of the Nationalist party and by C.K. Yen as president of the Republic of China. The position of chairman of the republic is abolished in China. Vietnam War ends with South Vietnam's surrender to North Vietnam.

1976 Jimmy Carter defeats Jerry Ford in presidential election in the U.S. Mao Zedong and Zhou Enlai die in China. Thirty high-ranking government and CCP members are arrested; Jiang Qing, Mao's widow and the leader of "Gang of Four" is also arrested. Hua Guofeng becomes premier and chairman of the CCP. North and South Vietnam are united as Socialist Republic of Vietnam with Hanoi as capital. U.S. and U.S.S.R. sign a nuclear arms limitation treaty.

1977 Winston Lord and Secretary of State Henry Kissinger are relieved of their diplomatic duties.

1978 Deng Xiaoping initiates agricultural reforms in China.

1979 Lords return to New York City. Many political prisoners are released from Chinese labor camps. China adopts One-Couple-One-Child policy to curb its population growth. U.S. and China establish full diplomatic ties. Beijing municipal government bans hanging of pro-democracy posters on the Democracy Wall. Margaret Thatcher becomes prime minister of Great Britain. Egypt and Israel sign the Camp David Accord. Islamic fundamentalists, under the leadership of the Ayatollah Ruhollah Khomeini, overthrow the Shah of Iran.

1980 Soviet forces invade Afghanistan. Ronald Reagan, a Republican, is elected president of the U.S.

1981 Bette publishes her second book *Spring Moon: A Novel of China*; it is later translated in eighteen languages. Winston Lord along with Kissinger joins the diplomatic services once again.

1982 Bette is nominated for American Book Award for her novel *Spring Moon: A Novel of China*. Bette receives an honorary Doctor of Laws (LLD) degree from Tufts University. IBM introduces its famous PC, or Personal Computer. According to the 1982 Chinese census, China's population reaches 1 billion. Nixon visits China to commemorate tenth anniversary of reinstatement of U.S.-Chinese relations. Argentina attempts to seize the Falkland Islands, but is defeated in air, sea, and land battles by Great Britain.

1983 Winston Lord is named senior counsellor of the President's National Bipartisan Commission on Central America. Chinese government launches a campaign to restrict foreign (Western) influence on culture and morality.

1984 Bette publishes *In The Year of the Boar and Jackie Robinson*, another successful book. Several industrial reforms are introduced in China.

1985 Bette receives the Jefferson Cup Award from American Library Association for *In The Year of the Boar and Jackie Robinson*. Winston Lord takes the post of U.S. Ambassador to People's Republic of China (til 1989). Mikhail Gorbachev becomes leader of the Soviet Union; he puts forward plans to change government through *perestroika* (reconstruction) and *glasnost* (openness).

1986 Bette's parents return to China for a visit after forty years. Soviet leader Gorbachev calls for better Chinese-Soviet relations. Chinese university students march to advocate democracy, human rights, and freedom.

1987 Bette receives Children's Book of the Year Award from Child Study Association of America for her book *In The Year of the Boar and Jackie Robinson*. Portugal and China sign an agreement to return the Portuguese colony of Macao to China in 1999. The Dalai Lama gives a speech for Tibetan independence before U.S. Congress. Martial law is lifted in Taiwan after 39 years of emergency rule. Pro-independence demonstration takes place in the Tibetan capital city of Lhasa.

1988 Bette and Winston celebrate their silver wedding anniversary in China. Chiang Ching-kuo, president of Taiwan, dies; he is succeeded by Lee Teng-hui. Sixteen Tibetan monks are killed in pro-independence riots. China relaxes its One-Couple-One-Child policy, allowing rural families to have second child if the first one is a girl. George Bush is elected president of the United States.

1989 Winston Lord finishes his assignment as U.S. Ambassador to China; Lords return to United States. Hu Yaobang, the former Communist party secretary, dies in China and is mourned by students; Chinese students struggle for democratic reforms; hundreds of people are killed and wounded in the Tiananmen Square massacre. Bette comes back to Beijing as a private citizen to act as interpreter for the CBS television crew covering Mikhail Gorbachev's visit to China. Bette writes another successful book *Legacies: A Chinese Mosaic*. Communism is rejected by country after country in Eastern Europe. Berlin Wall is officially opened.

1990 Former East and West Germany are united as Federal Republic of Germany. Mrs. Thatcher resigns as prime minister of Great Britain.

1991 Berlin is designated as the capital of Federal Republic of Germany. Jiang Quing, widow of Chairman Mao Zedong, commits suicide at the age of 77. Rajiv Gandhi, India's prime minister, is assassinated. Seven Chinese people accused of pro-democracy demonstration in 1989 are sentenced in China. Aung San Suu Kyi of Myanmar (Burma) receives Nobel Peace Prize.

1992 Three members of the Canadian Parliament are expelled from China by Chinese premier Li Peng. Menachem Begin, former prime minister of Israel, dies. Winston Lord is named assistant secretary for East Asian and Pacific affairs.

Forbidden City (Beijing), 53
Foreign Relations Subcommittee
  (U.S. Congress), 77
Ford, Gerald, 71
Freedom Forum, The, 97
Fulbright Exchange program, 39
Gate of Heavenly Peace, 94
Geneva, Switzerland, 49
"Goddess of Democracy," **88,** 94
Goo Ma (aunt), **62,** 65-66
Gorbachev, Mikhail, 90, 93, 94
Graham, Martha, 36, 50
grave sites, 66-67
Great Hall of the People, 90, 93
Guilin, China, 13
Guangdong, China, 67
Hangzhou, China, 67
Havel, Vaclav, **61**
Helms, Jesse, 77
Heston, Charlton, 84
Hong Kong, 41, 42, 89
Huangpu River, 68
Hummell, Arthur W., Jr., 75
Hu Yaobang, 89, 90
International Sugar Council, 40
Iran, hostage crisis, 73
Japanese, bombing of China by, 12
Jezebel, 11
Jiaotung College, 25
Jieu Jieu (Dora Bao's half brother),
  67, 68
John Paul II, Pope, 71
Kissinger, Henry, 47, 52, 67, 69, 73
Legacies: A Chinese Mosaic, 78, 82,
  85-86, 96
Lin Piao, 69
Li Peng, 94
Lord, Bette Bao: birth of, 9; tiger
  sign of, 10; naming of, 9-11;
  marriage of, 11, 45-46; as
  ambassador's wife in China, 11,
  75-87; writing career of, 11, 48-49,
  69-72, 74, 85-87, 96, 97; move to
  Hunan, 12-13; move to New York
  City, 15, 16-17, 19; English skills of,
  19-20, 22; as young immigrant,
  20-27; education of, 20-23, 26-27,
31-32, 34, 35, 36, 38; at Rapid
English Improvement (REI)
classes, 22; rules of family for,
22-23; and Chinese way of life,
25-26; family life of, 26-27; move
to New Jersey, 26, 31; friendships
of, 31, 32-33; first job of, 32; as
cashier in Chinese restaurant, 32;
relationship with Cathy, 32; and
Lutheran church, 33-34;
employment of, at insurance
company, 33; leadership skills of,
34; at Tufts University, 35; dance
classes for, 36, 49; at Fletcher
School of Law and Diplomacy, 36;
first meeting with Winston Lord,
36-37; move to Hawaii, 39;
employment of, at University of
Hawaii's East-West Cultural Center,
39; employment of, at Fulbright
Exchange program, 39, 47, 48;
engagement of, 39-40; raising of
family, 47-53; as author of *Eighth
Moon,* 48, 49; move to Geneva,
Switzerland, 49-50; as dance
instructor, 50; return to Washington,
51; trip to China, 63-69; reunion
with relatives, 63-68; interest in
photography, 68-69; return to U.S.,
69; move to Nederland, Colorado,
70; as author of *Spring Moon,*
69-72; as instant celebrity, 72-73;
return to New York City, 72-73; as
author of *Legacies: A Chinese
Mosaic,* 78, 82, 85-86, 96; as
author of *The Year of the Boar
and Jackie Robinson,* 74; as
interpreter and consultant to CBS,
89-90; visit to Hong Kong, 90; and
Tiananmen Square, 90-91; return
to U.S., 89-90; return to New York
City, 94-95; as member of Freedom
Forum, 97; as author of *The
Middle Heart,* 97
Lord, Bette Bao (illustrations), **4; 8,**
in a 1946 passport photo; **18,** in
1947; **28,** in Vermont in 1948; **54,**

106

ABOUT THE AUTHOR

Mary Virginia Fox was graduated from Northwestern University in Evanston, Illinois, and now lives near Madison, Wisconsin, located across the lake from the state capitol and the University of Wisconsin. She is the author of more than two dozen books for young adults and has had a number of articles published in adult publications. *Chief Joseph of the Nez Perce Indians: Champion of Liberty* also was written by Mrs. Fox.

Mrs. Fox and her husband have lived overseas for several months at a time and enjoy traveling. She considers herself a professional writer and an amateur artist.